foreword

As soon as we said we were gathering some of our best recipes for this handy cookbook about one of the world's favourite shellfish, the debate began: what's the difference between a shrimp and a prawn?

Some claim it has to do with size, and large shrimp are really prawns. But that doesn't explain how grocery stores can sell jumbo, or even colossal(!), shrimp. Others say shrimp live in salt water, while prawns inhabit fresh. But both migrate into each other's waters, so that's out. The name also depends on where they're eaten. In North America, it's a shrimp. In England and Australia, it's a prawn. What to do?

At Company's Coming, we've voted for shrimp. The name underlines the pleasing contrast between their tiny size and huge flavour. Dip into these pages and see—our collection of appetizers and entrees is simply *shrimp delicious!*

Jean Paré

surprise spread

You'll be tempted to eat this popular spread by the spoonful. An economical substitute for the cans of shrimp is 2 1/4 cups (550 mL) frozen small shrimp. Serve with tortilla chips or crackers.

Block of cream cheese, softened	8 oz.	250 g
Sour cream	1/2 cup	125 mL
Salad dressing (or mayonnaise)	1/4 cup	60 mL
Cans of small shrimp (4 oz., 106 g, each), rinsed and drained	3	3
Seafood cocktail sauce	1 cup	250 mL
Grated mozzarella cheese	2 cups	500 mL
Medium green pepper, chopped	1	1
Green onions, chopped	3	3
Medium tomato, diced	1	1

Mash first 3 ingredients with fork in small bowl. Spread evenly in ungreased 12 inch (30 cm) pizza pan or on serving platter.

Layer remaining 6 ingredients, in order given, over top. Chill, covered, until ready to serve. Serves 10.

1 serving: 286 Calories; 21.4 g Total Fat (7.3 g Mono, 2.4 g Poly, 10.4 g Sat); 107 mg Cholesterol; 9 g Carbohydrate; 1 g Fibre; 14 g Protein; 572 mg Sodium

simple shrimp dip

Easy peasy, lemon squeezy! Serve chips, crackers or raw vegetables as dippers.

Sour cream	2 cups	500 mL
Can of small shrimp, drained and mashed	4 oz.	106 g
Chili sauce (or ketchup)	1/4 cup	60 mL
Minced onion	1 tsp.	5 mL
Beef bouillon powder	1/2 tsp.	2 mL
Lemon juice	1/2 tsp.	2 mL
Worcestershire sauce	1/2 tsp.	2 mL

Combine all 7 ingredients in medium bowl. Chill for 1 hour. Makes about 2 1/2 cups (575 mL).

1 serving (2 tbsp., 30 mL): 51 Calories; 4.4 g Total Fat (1.3 g Mono, 0.2 g Poly, 2.7 g Sat); 23 mg Cholesterol; 1 g Carbohydrate; trace Fibre; 2 g Protein; 85 mg Sodium

curried shrimp tartlets

Be sure you have the rest of the meal ready when you serve these starters — they'll disappear quickly!

Frozen mini-tart shells	34	34
Hard margarine (or butter)	3 tbsp.	50 mL
All-purpose flour	3 tbsp.	50 mL
Milk	1 1/4 cups	300 mL
Anchovy paste	1 tsp.	5 mL
Curry powder	1 tsp.	5 mL
Granulated sugar	1 tsp.	5 mL
Salt	1/2 tsp.	2 mL
Pepper	1/8 tsp.	0.5 mL
Cooked small shrimp (peeled and deveined)	1/2 lb.	225 g

Paprika, sprinkle
Small sprigs of fresh parsley, for garnish

Arrange tartlet shells on 2 baking sheets with sides. Bake on separate racks in 375°F (190°C) oven for about 15 minutes, switching position of baking sheets at halftime, until golden.

Melt margarine in medium saucepan on medium. Sprinkle with flour. Heat and stir for 1 minute. Slowly add milk, stirring constantly, until smooth. Heat and stir until boiling and thickened.

Add next 5 ingredients. Stir. Cool.

Reserve 14 shrimp for garnish. Arrange remaining shrimp in shells. Spoon milk mixture over shrimp.

Sprinkle tartlets with paprika. Garnish with parsley sprigs and reserved shrimp. Chill for 1 to 2 hours until set. Makes 34 tartlets.

1 tartlet: 59 Calories; 3.5 g Total Fat (1.8 g Mono, 0.4 g Poly, 1.0 g Sat); 13 mg Cholesterol; 5 g Carbohydrate; trace Fibre; 2 g Protein; 120 mg Sodium

shrimp dumplings

These easy-to-make dumplings are the perfect appetizer for a dinner party, as they can be cooked ahead of time, chilled and reheated before serving.

Green onions, cut into 5 pieces each	3	3
Celery rib, cut into 5 pieces	1	1
Uncooked medium shrimp (peeled and deveined)	3/4 lb.	340 g
Egg white (large)	1	1
Cornstarch	2 tbsp.	30 mL
Soy sauce	2 tbsp.	30 mL
Sesame (or cooking) oil	1 tsp.	5 mL
Hot pepper sauce	1/4 tsp.	1 mL
Chopped fresh cilantro or parsley (optional)	1/4 cup	60 mL
Round dumpling wrappers, thawed	30	30
Sesame seeds, toasted (see Tip, page 64)	1 1/2 tsp.	7 mL
Cooking oil	2 tbsp.	30 mL
Hot water	1 1/2 cups	375 mL

Put green onion and celery into food processor. Process with on/off motion until finely chopped. Add shrimp. Process with on/off motion until chopped.

Add next 6 ingredients. Process until well mixed and consistency of thick paste.

Dampen edge of 1 wrapper with water. Place 1 tbsp. (15 mL) shrimp mixture in centre. Bring edge of wrapper up towards centre. Pinch into 4 or 5 folds, leaving small opening. Repeat with remaining wrappers and shrimp mixture. Sprinkle opening with sesame seeds.

Heat 2 tsp. (10 mL) cooking oil in large non-stick frying pan on medium. Add dumplings, 8 to 10 at a time. Carefully pour 1/2 cup (125 mL) hot water into pan around dumplings. Cook, covered, for 5 to 8 minutes until dumplings are browned on bottom and liquid is evaporated. Repeat with remaining dumplings, oil and water. Makes 30 dumplings. Serves 10.

1 serving: 198 Calories; 4.5 g Total Fat (2 g Mono, 1.5 g Poly, 0.5 g Sat); 37 mg Cholesterol; 29 g Carbohydrate; trace Fibre; 10 g Protein; 513 mg Sodium

shrimp in beer batter

The beer in this recipe creates a lighter batter and a crispier texture.

All-purpose flour	1 cup	250 mL
Beer	1 cup	250 mL
Cooking oil	2 tbsp.	30 mL
Salt	1 tsp.	5 mL
Egg white (large)	1	1
Uncooked large shrimp (peeled and deveined), tails intact	1 lb.	454 g
Cooking oil, for deep-frying		
HONEY MUSTARD DIPPING SAUCE		
Dijon mustard (with whole seeds)	1/4 cup	60 mL
Liquid honey	3 tbsp.	50 mL

Combine first 4 ingredients in large bowl. Let stand, covered, for 1 hour.

Beat egg white in small bowl until soft peaks form. Fold into batter until no white streaks remain.

Holding shrimp by tail, dip straight down into batter allowing excess to drip back into bowl. Deep-fry, in 2 to 3 batches, in hot (375°F, 190°C) cooking oil for about 3 minutes per batch until golden. Remove each batch to paper towels to drain.

Honey Mustard Dipping Sauce: Combine mustard and honey in separate small bowl. Makes about 1/3 cup (75 mL) sauce. Serve with shrimp. Makes about 21 to 30 shrimp.

1 shrimp with about 3/4 tsp. (4 mL) sauce: 96 Calories; 4.3 g Total Fat (2.2 g Mono, 1.4 g Poly, 0.4 g Sat); 33 mg Cholesterol; 8 g Carbohydrate; trace Fibre; 5 g Protein; 189 mg Sodium

shrimp spring rolls

A bowl of soy sauce, with an optional grating of fresh ginger, pairs well with these delicious spring rolls. Garnish with thinly sliced carrots and cucumber.

Uncooked shrimp (peeled and deveined), blotted dry and finely chopped	1/2 lb.	225 g
Finely chopped green onion (or cilantro)	1 tbsp.	15 mL
Finely grated carrot	1 tbsp.	15 mL
Cornstarch	2 tsp.	10 mL
Low-sodium soy sauce	2 tsp.	10 mL
Sesame seeds, toasted (see Tip, page 64)	1 tsp.	5 mL
Finely grated gingerroot	1/2 tsp.	2 mL
Granulated sugar	1/2 tsp.	2 mL
Garlic clove, minced	1/2	1/2
Water	2 tbsp.	30 mL
All-purpose flour	1 tbsp.	15 mL
Spring roll wrappers (8 1/2 inch, 21 cm, square)	9	9

Peanut (or cooking) oil, for deep-frying

Combine first 9 ingredients in small bowl.

Stir water into flour in small cup until smooth.

Lay wrappers on top of each other. Cut wrappers in half, making 18 rectangles. Place 1 wrapper on work surface with short side closest to you. Cover remaining sheets with damp towel to prevent drying. Brush all 4 edges of wrapper with flour mixture. Place about 2 tsp. (10 mL) shrimp mixture at centre of short end, about 1/2 inch (12 mm) from edge. Fold bottom edge of wrapper over shrimp mixture. Fold in sides. Roll up from bottom to enclose filling. Repeat with remaining shrimp mixture and rectangles.

Deep-fry spring rolls, in 3 batches, in hot (375°F, 190°C) peanut oil for about 3 minutes per batch, turning often, until crisp and golden. Remove each batch to paper towels to drain. Makes 18 spring rolls.

3 spring rolls: 291 Calories; 8.6 g Total Fat (3.5 g Mono, 2.9 g Poly, 1.5 g Sat); 49 mg Cholesterol; 40 g Carbohydrate; trace Fibre; 12 g Protein; 463 mg Sodium

barbecued shrimp

Perfectly marinated and barbecued shrimp are served with an easy, garlicky aioli. A fast way to thaw frozen shrimp is to place them in a colander under cold running water.

AIOLI

Mayonnaise (not salad dressing)	1/2 cup	125 mL
Chopped fresh parsley (or 1/4 tsp., 1 mL, flakes)	1 tsp.	5 mL
Garlic clove, minced (or 1/8 tsp., 0.5 mL, powder)	1/2	1/2

SHRIMP

Chopped fresh parsley (or 2 1/4 tsp., 11 mL, flakes)	3 tbsp.	50 mL
Cooking oil	2 tbsp.	30 mL
Grated lemon zest	1/2 tsp.	2 mL
Salt	1/2 tsp.	2 mL
Pepper	1/2 tsp.	2 mL
Uncooked extra-large shrimp (peeled and deveined), tails intact	18	18

Aioli: Combine all 3 ingredients in small bowl. Chill, covered, for 30 minutes to blend flavours.

Shrimp: Combine first 5 ingredients in medium bowl.

Add shrimp. Toss until coated. Let stand, covered, in refrigerator for 1 hour, stirring occasionally. Drain and discard liquid. Preheat gas barbecue to medium. Cook shrimp on greased grill for about 5 minutes, turning occasionally, until shrimp turn pink. Serve with Aioli. Serves 6.

1 serving: 197 Calories; 19.6 g Total Fat (2.7 g Mono, 1.5 g Poly, 2.4 g Sat); 39 mg Cholesterol; 1 g Carbohydrate; trace Fibre; 4 g Protein; 347 mg Sodium

thai shrimp cocktails

A far cry from that half-frozen ring of shrimp on a plastic dish! This update with Thai flavours of curry, sweet chili and lime can be refrigerated in an air-tight container for up to 24 hours. You can also assemble, cover and chill these cocktails up to eight hours before serving.

Cooking oil	1 tbsp.	15 mL
Garlic cloves, minced (or 1/2 tsp., 2 mL, powder)	2	2
Finely grated gingerroot	1 tsp.	5 mL
Red curry paste	1 tsp.	5 mL
Bags of uncooked shrimp (3/4 lb., 340 g, each), peeled, deveined, and coarsely chopped	2	2
Lime juice	2 tbsp.	30 mL
Sweet chili sauce	2 tbsp.	30 mL
Fish sauce (or soy sauce)	1 tbsp.	15 mL
Fresh bean sprouts	1 cup	250 mL
Coarsely chopped unsalted peanuts	1/2 cup	125 mL
Coarsely chopped fresh cilantro or parsley	1/4 cup	60 mL
Butter lettuce leaves	24	24

Heat cooking oil in large frying pan on medium. Add next 3 ingredients. Heat and stir for 1 to 2 minutes until fragrant.

Add next 4 ingredients. Heat and stir for about 3 minutes until shrimp turn pink. Remove from heat.

Add next 3 ingredients. Stir. Transfer to medium bowl. Chill for about 1 hour until cold.

Press lettuce leaves into 12 small wine glasses. Spoon shrimp mixture over lettuce. Makes 12 shrimp cocktails.

1 shrimp cocktail: 121 Calories; 5.6 g Total Fat (2.5 g Mono, 1.8 g Poly, 0.7 g Sat); 86 mg Cholesterol; 4 g Carbohydrate; 1 g Fibre; 14 g Protein; 166 mg Sodium

chili lemon shrimp

A great combination of flavours works its magic on these broiled jumbo shrimp. You can also cook these on a pre-heated electric grill or barbecue for two minutes per side, basting them with the boiled marinade. Don't overcook!

Chopped fresh parsley (or 2 tbsp., 30 mL, flakes)	2/3 cup	150 mL
Dry (or alcohol-free) white wine	2/3 cup	150 mL
Shallots (or green onions), finely chopped	2	2
Lemon juice	1/4 cup	60 mL
Sweet (or regular) chili sauce	1/4 cup	60 mL
Liquid honey	3 tbsp.	50 mL
Olive (or cooking) oil	2 tbsp.	30 mL
Dried crushed chilies	2 tsp.	10 mL
Grated lemon zest	1 tsp.	5 mL
Seasoned salt	1 tsp.	5 mL
Uncooked extra-large shrimp (peeled and deveined), tails intact (25 to 30 shrimp)	2 1/4 lbs.	1 kg
Bamboo skewers (4 inches, 10 cm, each), soaked in water for 10 minutes	25 – 30	25 – 30

Combine first 10 ingredients in large bowl.

Add shrimp. Stir until coated. Let stand, covered, in refrigerator for 3 hours, stirring occasionally. Drain, reserving wine mixture in small saucepan. Bring to a boil. Reduce heat to medium. Boil gently, uncovered, for at least 5 minutes.

Thread 1 shrimp, starting at head end, lengthwise onto each skewer. Place on greased broiler pan. Broil on top rack in oven for about 2 minutes per side, brushing with wine mixture several times, until shrimp turn pink. Makes 25 to 30 shrimp.

1 shrimp: 72 Calories; 1.9 g Total Fat (0.9 g Mono, 0.4 g Poly, 0.3 g Sat); 61 mg Cholesterol; 4 g Carbohydrate; trace Fibre; 8 g Protein; 150 mg Sodium

coconut shrimp

Assemble the shrimp skewers up to four hours ahead of time and chill in an airtight container. Bake these a dozen at a time so guests can enjoy hot hors d'oeuvres throughout the evening. The sauce can be made up to a day ahead.

Uncooked medium shrimp (peeled and deveined)	48	48
Bamboo skewers (4 inches, 10 cm, each), soaked in water for 10 minutes	48	48
All-purpose flour	1/3 cup	75 mL
Salt	1/8 tsp.	0.5 mL
Large eggs	2	2
Chili paste (sambal oelek)	2 tbsp.	30 mL
Shredded (long thread) coconut	2 cups	500 mL
Cooking spray		
THAI DIPPING SAUCE		
Sweet chili sauce	3/4 cup	175 mL
Chopped fresh cilantro or parsley	3 tbsp.	50 mL
Lime juice	3 tbsp.	50 mL

Thread 1 shrimp, starting at tail end, lengthwise onto each skewer. Set aside.

Combine flour and salt in small shallow dish.

Beat eggs and chili paste in separate small shallow dish.

Measure coconut into third small shallow dish. Holding 1 skewer, press both sides of shrimp in flour mixture until coated. Dip shrimp into egg mixture. Press into coconut until coated. Place on greased parchment paper-lined baking sheet. Repeat with remaining shrimp skewers.

Spray shrimp with cooking spray. Bake in 425°F (220°C) oven for about 8 minutes, turning once, until coconut is golden and shrimp are firm and pink.

Thai Dipping Sauce: Combine all 3 ingredients in small bowl. Makes about 1 cup (250 mL) sauce. Serve with shrimp. Makes 48 skewers.

1 skewer with 1 tsp. (5 mL) sauce: 35 Calories; 1.4 g Total Fat (0.2 g Mono, 0.1 g Poly, 1.0 g Sat); 20 mg Cholesterol; 4 g Carbohydrate; trace Fibre; 2 g Protein; 89 mg Sodium

shrimp salad rolls

The Chinese vermicelli in this dish is sometimes called cellophane noodles.
Let your guests get involved by having them roll their own appetizers.

CHILI MAYONNAISE

Mayonnaise (not salad dressing)	1/3 cup	75 mL
Plain yogurt	1/4 cup	60 mL
Seafood cocktail sauce	2 tbsp.	30 mL
Finely chopped green onion	1 tbsp.	15 mL
Chili paste (sambal oelek)	2 tsp.	10 mL

FILLING

Chinese-style vermicelli (bean thread),or rice vermicelli, broken up	2 oz.	57 g
Boiling water		
Water	2 tbsp.	30 mL
Cornstarch	2 tsp.	10 mL
Chili sauce	1 tbsp.	15 mL
Dry sherry	1 tbsp.	15 mL
Hoisin sauce	1 tbsp.	15 mL
Granulated sugar	1 tsp.	5 mL
Sesame oil (for flavour)	1 tsp.	5 mL
Salt	1/2 tsp.	2 mL
Cooking oil	2 tbsp.	30 mL
Finely chopped broccoli	1 cup	250 mL
Grated carrot	1/4 cup	60 mL
Finely grated gingerroot (or 1/4 tsp., 1 mL, ground ginger)	1 tsp.	5 mL
Garlic clove, minced (or 1/4 tsp., 1 mL, powder)	1	1
Uncooked medium shrimp (peeled and deveined), chopped	1/2 lb.	225 g
Green onions, sliced	2	2
Butter (or iceberg) lettuce leaves	24	24

Chili Mayonnaise: Combine all 5 ingredients in small bowl. Chill, covered, for 1 hour. Makes about 2/3 cup (150 mL) mayonnaise.

Filling: Put vermicelli into medium heatproof bowl. Cover with boiling water. Let stand for about 5 minutes until softened. Drain well. Transfer to large bowl. Set aside.

Stir water into cornstarch in small bowl. Add next 6 ingredients. Stir. Set aside.

Heat wok or large frying pan on medium-high until very hot. Add cooking oil. Add next 4 ingredients. Stir-fry for 1 minute.

Add shrimp and green onion. Stir-fry for 2 to 3 minutes until shrimp turn pink. Stir cornstarch mixture. Add to shrimp mixture. Stir-fry for 1 to 2 minutes until boiling and thickened. Add to vermicelli. Toss. Transfer to serving plate. Makes about 3 cups (750 mL) filling.

Place lettuce leaves in stacks around filling. To assemble, place about 2 tbsp. (30 mL) filling in centre of each lettuce leaf. Roll up to enclose filling. Serve with Chili Mayonnaise. Serves 6.

1 serving: 259 Calories; 16.9 g Total Fat (8.9 g Mono, 5.5 g Poly, 1.7 g Sat); 65 mg Cholesterol; 17g Carbohydrate; 1 g Fibre; 10 g Protein; 508 mg Sodium

coconut seafood cakes
with mango salsa

Packed with exotic flavours, these crisp little appetizers will disappear in a hurry. Garnish with cilantro.

Large egg, fork-beaten	1	1
Can of coconut milk	14 oz.	398 mL
Fish sauce	1 tbsp.	15 mL
Green curry paste	1 tbsp.	15 mL
Uncooked shrimp (peeled and deveined), finely chopped	8 oz.	225 g
Can of crabmeat, drained, cartilage removed, flaked	4 1/4 oz.	120 g
All-purpose flour	1 cup	250 mL
Baking powder	1 tsp.	5 mL
Cooking oil	2 tbsp.	30 mL

MANGO SALSA

Small mangoes, pitted, peeled, finely chopped	2	2
Small Roma (plum) tomatoes, seeds removed, finely chopped	4	4
Green onions, finely chopped	3	3
Chopped fresh cilantro or parsley (or 2 1/4 tsp., 11 mL flakes)	3 tbsp.	50 mL
Sweet chili sauce	2 tbsp.	30 mL
Balsamic vinegar	1 tbsp.	15 mL

Combine first 4 ingredients in medium bowl. Add shrimp and crabmeat. Stir. Add flour and baking powder. Stir until smooth.

Heat 2 tsp. (10 mL) cooking oil in large shallow frying pan on medium. Drop seafood mixture, 2 1/2 tbsp. (37 mL) at a time, about 4 inches apart, onto hot pan. Spread to form 3 inch (7.5 cm) cakes. Cook for about 3 minutes per side until lightly browned. Remove to large serving plate. Cover to keep warm. Repeat with remaining seafood mixture and oil. Makes about 24 cakes.

Mango Salsa: Combine all 6 ingredients in medium bowl. Makes about 4 cups (1 L) salsa. Serve with Seafood Cakes. Place 3 or 4 cakes on 8 individual plates. Spoon salsa over top. Serves 6.

1 serving: 463 Calories; 30.6 g Total Fat (9.7 g Mono, 5.1 g Poly, 13.6 g Sat); 93 mg Cholesterol; 34 g Carbohydrate; 3 g Fibre; 17 g Protein; 528 mg Sodium

beacon shrimp omelette

Nanaimo, British Columbia, isn't just known for its gooey, chocolatey squares. The inspiration for this much-loved, shrimp-stuffed omelette, flavoured with horseradish and lemon juice occurred in one of the city's apartment buildings, called The Beacon.

SEAFOOD SAUCE:		
Ketchup	3 tbsp.	50 mL
Lemon juice	1 1/2 tsp.	7 mL
Creamed horseradish	1 tsp.	5 mL
Worcestershire sauce	1/4 tsp.	1 mL

OMELETTE		
Large eggs, fork-beaten	2	2
Light cream cheese, cut up and softened	3 tbsp.	50 mL
Cooked baby shrimp	1/3 cup	75 mL
Chopped green onion	2 tbsp.	30 mL
Chopped chives, for garnish		

Seafood Sauce: Combine all 4 ingredients in small bowl. Makes about 3 tbsp. (50 mL) sauce.

Omelette: Spray small (8 inch, 20 cm) non-stick frying pan with cooking spray. Heat on medium until hot. Pour eggs into pan. Reduce heat to medium-low. When starting to set at outside edge, tilt pan and gently lift cooked egg with spatula, easing around pan from outside edge in. Allow uncooked egg to flow onto bottom of pan until egg is softly set.

Scatter cream cheese over half of omelette. Drizzle Seafood Sauce over cheese. Sprinkle with shrimp and green onion. Cook, covered, on low for 1 to 2 minutes until cheese is melted and shrimp are hot. Slide onto plate, folding omelette in half over filling. Garnish with chives. Serves 1.

1 serving: 363 Calories; 19.8 g Total Fat (7.4 g Mono, 2.1 g Poly, 7.8 g Sat); 541 mg Cholesterol; 19 g Carbohydrate; 1 g Fibre; 28 g Protein; 1309 mg Sodium

shrimp quiche

Need something to bring along to a spring brunch? Let this colourful quiche cool before covering, then reheat in a 325°F (160°C) oven for 30 minutes until heated through.

Cooked medium shrimp (peeled and deveined), blotted dry	4 oz.	113 g
Unbaked 9 inch (22 cm) pie shell	1	1
Grated Swiss cheese	1 cup	250 mL
Green onions, thinly sliced	4	4
Large eggs	3	3
Mayonnaise	1/2 cup	125 mL
Milk	1/2 cup	125 mL
All-purpose flour	2 tbsp.	30 mL
Chopped pimiento	2 tbsp.	30 mL
Chopped fresh dill (or 1/4 tsp., 1 mL, dried)	1 tsp.	5 mL
Curry powder	1/2 tsp.	2 mL
Salt	1/4 tsp.	1 mL

Reserve 3 shrimp for garnish. Scatter remaining shrimp in pie shell. Scatter cheese and green onion over shrimp. Set aside.

Beat eggs in medium bowl until frothy. Beat in next 7 ingredients. Pour into pie shell. Top with reserved shrimp. Bake on bottom rack in 350°F (175°C) oven for about 40 minutes until knife inserted in centre comes out clean. Let stand for 10 minutes before serving. Cuts into 6 wedges.

1 wedge: 400 Calories; 30.8 g Total Fat (14.4 g Mono, 6.7 g Poly, 8.1g Sat); 166 mg Cholesterol; 15 g Carbohydrate; trace Fibre; 15 g Protein; 457 mg Sodium

egg roll with shrimp

Here's an egg roll with a twist—no deep-frying involved! Serve with extra cocktail sauce.

Large eggs, fork beaten	3	3
Milk	2/3 cup	150 mL
Creamed horseradish	2 tsp.	10 mL
Salt	1/2 tsp.	2 mL
All-purpose flour	1/3 cup	75 mL
Hard margarine (or butter)	1 tbsp.	15 mL
Grated mozzarella cheese	3/4 cup	175 mL
Cooked small shrimp (peeled and deveined), blotted dry	6 oz.	170 g
Medium Roma (plum) tomatoes, seeds removed and diced	2	2
Finely diced celery	1/4 cup	60 mL
Green onions, sliced	2	2
Salt, sprinkle		
Pepper, sprinkle		
Spicy cocktail sauce	2 tbsp.	30 mL
Sharp Cheddar cheese, cut into 4 strips	2 oz.	57 g

Beat first 4 ingredients in medium bowl until smooth. Add flour. Stir until smooth.

Melt margarine in 9 x 13 inch (22 x 33 cm) pan in 350°F (175°C) oven for about 2 minutes until bubbling. Pour egg mixture into pan. Bake, uncovered, for 25 to 30 minutes until set and lightly browned. Run spatula around inside edges of pan to loosen egg mixture. Invert onto baking sheet.

Sprinkle next 7 ingredients over egg mixture.

Randomly spoon dabs of cocktail sauce over shrimp. Roll up, jelly roll-style, from long side. Place seam-side down on same baking sheet. Arrange Cheddar cheese on top of roll. Bake in 350°F (175°C) oven for 8 to 10 minutes until Cheddar cheese is melted. Cuts into 8 diagonal slices. Serves 4.

1 serving: 331 Calories; 18 g Total Fat (6.5 g Mono, 1.6 g Poly, 8.3 g Sat); 261 mg Cholesterol; 17 g Carbohydrate; 1 g Fibre; 25 g Protein; 749 mg Sodium

shrimp brie croissants

Soft pieces of Brie add a touch of sophistication to this delicious shrimp filling. Serve with a bowl of soup for a satisfying lunch. You can store the shrimp mixture in the fridge for up to 24 hours.

Cooked shrimp (peeled and deveined), blotted dry, chopped	1/2 cup	125 mL
Brie cheese, chopped	1 1/2 oz.	43 g
Mayonnaise	1 tbsp.	15 mL
Seafood cocktail sauce	1 tbsp.	15 mL
Mini croissants, split	6	6
Lettuce leaves (your choice), halved	3	3

Combine first 4 ingredients in small bowl.

Spread shrimp mixture over bottom half of each croissant.

Place lettuce on shrimp mixture. Cover with top halves of croissants. Makes 6 croissants.

1 croissant: 192 Calories; 10.9 g Total Fat (3.5 g Mono, 1.2 g Poly, 5.3 g Sat); 62 mg Cholesterol; 16 g Carbohydrate; 1 g Fibre; 7 g Protein; 367 mg Sodium

seafood focaccia loaf

This appetizing dish serves up well for brunch or lunch, but would also star as a half-time treat.

Herb focaccia bread (about 8 inch, 20 cm, round)	1	1
Basil pesto	1/4 cup	60 mL
Olive (or cooking) oil	1 tsp.	5 mL
Diced fresh white mushrooms	1/2 cup	125 mL
Diced green pepper	1/2 cup	125 mL
Diced onion	1/2 cup	125 mL
Garlic clove, minced (or 1/4 tsp., 1 mL, powder)	1	1
Olive (or cooking) oil	1 tsp.	5 mL
Uncooked medium shrimp (peeled and deveined)	4 oz.	113 g
Uncooked small bay scallops	4 oz.	113 g
Crumbled feta cheese	1/2 cup	125 mL
Diced black olives (or seasoned black Italian olives)	2 tbsp.	30 mL

Cut bread in half horizontally. Spread pesto on cut sides of bread. Place, cut-side up, on ungreased baking sheet.

Heat first amount of olive oil in medium frying pan on medium-high. Add next 4 ingredients. Cook for about 5 minutes, stirring often, until onion is softened. Spread on bottom half of bread.

Heat second amount of olive oil in same frying pan. Add scallops and shrimp. Stir-fry for 2 to 3 minutes until scallops are opaque and shrimp turn pink. Scatter over vegetable mixture.

Sprinkle cheese and olives over seafood mixture. Bake in 350°F (175°C) oven for 15 to 20 minutes until edges are crusty. Place top half of focaccia bread over seafood mixture. Press down gently. Cut into wedges. Serves 4.

1 serving: 406 Calories; 14 g Total Fat (7.0 g Mono, 1.4 g Poly, 4.4 g Sat); 70 mg Cholesterol; 49 g Carbohydrate; 3 g Fibre; 20 g Protein; 659 mg Sodium

shrimp and mango salad

The delicious combination of mango and shrimp will have your guests coming back for seconds. Store leftover peanuts in the fridge to keep them fresh.

Uncooked large shrimp (peeled and deveined), tails intact	1/2 lb.	225 g
Hard margarine (or butter), melted	3 tbsp.	50 mL
Garlic clove, minced (or 1/4 tsp., 1 mL, powder)	1	1
Salt	1/4 tsp.	1 mL
Pepper, sprinkle		
Can of sliced mango in syrup, drained and coarsely chopped	14 oz.	398 mL
Salted peanuts	1/2 cup	125 mL
Fresh spinach leaves, lightly packed	5 cups	1.25 L
PEANUT OIL VINAIGRETTE		
Peanut (or cooking) oil	3 tbsp.	50 mL
White wine vinegar	2 tbsp.	30 mL
Brown sugar, packed	2 tsp.	10 mL
Salt	1/4 tsp.	1 mL
Pepper, just a pinch		

Cut shrimp along back, halfway through to other side. Put into large bowl.

Add next 4 ingredients. Toss until coated. Preheat gas barbecue to medium. Cook shrimp on greased grill for 3 to 5 minutes, turning occasionally, until pink.

Put next 3 ingredients and shrimp into separate large bowl. Toss.

Peanut Oil Vinaigrette: Combine all 5 ingredients in jar with tight-fitting lid. Shake well. Makes about 1/2 cup (125 mL) vinaigrette. Drizzle over shrimp mixture. Makes about 8 cups (2 L). Serves 8.

1 serving: 196 Calories; 14.8 g Total Fat (7.7 g Mono, 3.8 g Poly, 2.5 g Sat); 32 mg Cholesterol; 10 g Carbohydrate; 2 g Fibre; 7 g Protein; 327 mg Sodium

tomato shrimp soup

A squeeze bottle lets you make interesting patterns with the Basil Vinaigrette. The soup will keep in the fridge for three days, and in the freezer for a month. The vinaigrette can be refrigerated for up to three days.

Olive (or cooking) oil	1 tsp.	5 mL
Uncooked small shrimp (peeled and deveined)	1 lb.	454 g
Olive (or cooking) oil	1 tsp.	5 mL
Finely chopped onion	1 cup	250 mL
Finely chopped fennel bulb (white part only)	1/2 cup	125 mL
Garlic clove, minced (or 1/4 tsp., 1 mL, powder)	1	1
Licorice-flavoured liqueur	2 tbsp.	30 mL
Cans of crushed tomatoes (28 oz., 796 mL, each)	2	2
Prepared chicken broth	3 3/4 cups	925 mL
Water	1 1/4 cups	300 mL

BASIL VINAIGRETTE

Chopped fresh basil	1 cup	250 mL
Olive (or cooking) oil	1/2 cup	125 mL
White wine vinegar	3 tbsp.	50 mL
Liquid honey	1 tbsp.	15 mL
Salt, just a pinch		
Pepper, just a pinch		

Heat first amount of olive oil in large saucepan on medium-high. Add shrimp. Heat and stir for about 1 minute until shrimp turn pink. Transfer to large bowl. Set aside. Reduce heat to medium.

Heat second amount of olive oil in same pot. Add next 3 ingredients. Cook for about 5 minutes, stirring often, until onion is softened.

Add liqueur. Heat and stir for 1 minute.

Add next 3 ingredients. Stir. Bring to a boil. Reduce heat to medium-low. Simmer, covered, for about 20 minutes, stirring occasionally, until fennel is tender. Add shrimp. Cook for about 2 minutes until shrimp are heated through.

Basil Vinaigrette: Process all 6 ingredients in blender or food processor until smooth. Makes about 1 cup (250 mL) vinaigrette. Drizzle on individual servings. Serves 8.

1 serving: 302 Calories; 16.8 g Total Fat (11.2 g Mono, 2.0 g Poly, 2.4 g Sat); 86 mg Cholesterol; 24 g Carbohydrate; 5 Fibre; 16 g Protein; 1054 mg Sodium

shrimp and mushroom soup

Easy, elegant soups are wonderful dinner-party staples. Make this up to two days ahead and chill. Reheat gently on low.

Hard margarine (or butter)	1 tbsp.	15 mL
Chopped fresh white mushrooms	2 cups	500 mL
Finely chopped onion	1/3 cup	75 mL
All-purpose flour	1/4 cup	60 mL
Dry mustard	1/2 tsp.	2 mL
Garlic salt	1/4 tsp.	1 mL
Salt	1/2 tsp.	2 mL
Pepper	1/8 tsp.	0.5 mL
Can of skim evaporated milk	13 1/2 oz.	385 mL
Milk	1 1/3 cups	325 mL
Water	1 cup	250 mL
Sweet sherry (optional)	1 tbsp.	15 mL
Cans of cocktail shrimp (with liquid), 4 oz., 106 g, each	2	2

Melt margarine in large frying pan on medium. Add mushrooms and onion. Cook for 5 minutes, stirring often, until onion is softened and liquid is evaporated.

Add next 5 ingredients. Heat and stir for 1 minute.

Slowly add next 3 ingredients, stirring constantly. Heat and stir until boiling and thickened. Add sherry. Stir.

Add shrimp with liquid. Stir. Cook for about 2 minutes until heated through. Makes about 5 cups (1.25 L).

1 cup (250 mL): 206 Calories; 4.4 g Total Fat (2.0 g Mono, 0.7 g Poly, 1.2 g Sat); 84 mg Cholesterol; 21 g Carbohydrate; 1 g Fibre; 20 g Protein; 577 mg Sodium

creamy seafood soup

Shallow bowls will keep your heart-shaped garnish afloat!

Hard margarine (or butter)	1 tbsp.	15 mL
Uncooked large sea scallops (8 – 10)	6 oz.	170 g
Uncooked medium shrimp (peeled and deveined)	6 oz.	170 g
Cooking oil	1 tbsp.	15 mL
Chopped onion	1/3 cup	75 mL
Garlic clove, minced (or 1/4 tsp., 1 mL, powder)	1	1
All-purpose flour	2 tsp.	10 mL
Dry (or alcohol-free) white wine	1/4 cup	60 mL
Prepared chicken broth	1 cup	250 mL
Salt	1/8 tsp.	0.5 mL
Pepper, sprinkle		
Whipping cream (or half-and-half cream)	1/2 cup	125 mL
Chopped fresh chives, for garnish		

Melt margarine in medium saucepan on medium. Add scallops and shrimp. Cook for about 3 minutes, stirring occasionally, until scallops are opaque and shrimp turn pink. Reserve 4 shrimp. Keep warm. Transfer remaining seafood mixture to small plate.

Heat cooking oil in same saucepan on medium. Add onion and garlic. Cook for about 5 minutes, stirring often, until onion is softened.

Sprinkle with flour. Heat and stir for 1 minute. Slowly add wine. Heat and stir for 1 to 2 minutes until boiling and thickened. Add next 3 ingredients. Stir. Bring to a boil. Reduce heat to medium-low. Simmer, uncovered, for 3 to 5 minutes until thickened. Remove from heat.

Add whipping cream. Add reserved seafood mixture. Carefully process with hand blender or in blender until smooth. Makes about 2 1/3 cups (575 mL) soup.

Garnish individual servings with reserved shrimp and chives. Serves 2.

1 serving: 504 Calories; 35.4 g Total Fat (14.3 g Mono, 4 g Poly, 14.8 g Sat); 187 mg Cholesterol; 10 g Carbohydrate; 1 g Fibre; 31 g Protein; 881 mg Sodium

seafood ravioli with dill-and-caper butter sauce

These sumptuous pasta pouches can be made a day ahead and placed in single layers on baking sheets dusted with cornstarch (to absorb any moisture that may seep through the wrappers). Wrap tightly and chill until you're ready to cook them.

Uncooked medium shrimp (peeled and deveined)	12 1/2 oz.	350 g
Uncooked sea scallops	6 oz.	170 g
Chopped fresh chives (or 1 1/2 tsp., 7 mL dried)	2 tbsp.	30 mL
Goat (chèvre) cheese, cut-up (about 2 oz., 57 g)	1/4 cup	60 mL
Garlic clove, crushed (or 1/4 tsp., 1 mL, powder)	1	1
Grated lemon zest	1/2 tsp.	2 mL
Salt	1/4 tsp.	1 mL
Pepper	1/2 tsp.	2 mL
Round dumpling wrappers	40	40
Large egg	1	1
Water	1 tbsp.	15 mL
Water	10 cups	2.5 L
Salt	1 tsp.	5 mL

DILL-AND-CAPER BUTTER SAUCE

Butter	2/3 cup	150 mL
Capers, coarsely chopped	2 tbsp.	30 mL
Chopped fresh dill (or 1 1/2 tsp., 7 mL, dried)	2 tbsp.	30 mL
Chopped pecans	2 tbsp.	30 mL
Salt	1/4 tsp.	1 mL
Pepper	1/2 tsp.	2 mL

Process first 8 ingredients in food processor until coarsely chopped.

Whisk egg and first amount of water in small bowl. Place 1 1/2 tbsp. (25 mL) filling in centre of 1 wrapper. Brush edges of wrapper with egg mixture. Place second wrapper over filling. Press edges together to seal. Repeat with remaining filling and wrappers.

Combine second amount of water and salt in large saucepan. Bring to a boil. Add ravioli in 2 batches. Boil, uncovered, for about 5 minutes per batch, stirring occasionally, until tender but firm. Drain. Makes 20 ravioli.

Dill-and-Caper Butter Sauce: Melt butter in medium frying pan on medium. Add remaining 5 ingredients. Heat and stir for 3 to 5 minutes until butter is lightly browned. Makes about 1/2 cup (125 mL) sauce. Arrange 5 ravioli on each of 4 side plates. Drizzle with butter sauce. Serves 4.

1 serving: 725 Calories; 40.8 g Total Fat (12.0 g Mono, 3.2 g Poly, 22.5 g Sat); 301 mg Cholesterol; 50 g Carbohydrate; trace Fibre; 38 g Protein; 1371 mg Sodium

shrimp mango curry

Choose a ripe mango with rich red and/or yellow colouring and only a hint of green. It should yield slightly to gentle pressure. Its sweetness will contrast beautifully with the curry paste and sambal oelek in this dish. Delicious served over rice.

Hard margarine (or butter)	1 tbsp.	15 mL
Medium ripe mango, chopped	1	1
Chopped celery	3/4 cup	175 mL
Diced onion	1/2 cup	125 mL
Garlic clove, minced (or 1/4 tsp., 1 mL, powder)	1	1
All-purpose flour	3 tbsp.	50 mL
Curry paste (or 3/4 tsp., 4 mL, powder)	1 1/2 tsp.	7 mL
Chili paste (sambal oelek)	1 tsp.	5 mL
Prepared chicken broth	2 cups	500 mL
Coconut milk (or reconstituted from powder)	1 1/3 cups	325 mL
Dark raisins	1/2 cup	125 mL
Uncooked large shrimp (peeled and deveined) tails intact	1 1/2 lbs.	680 g
Brown sugar, packed	1 tbsp.	15 mL
Salt	1/4 tsp.	1 mL

Heat wok or large frying pan on medium-high until very hot. Add margarine. Add next 4 ingredients. Stir-fry for about 5 minutes until onion is softened

Add next 3 ingredients. Stir-fry for 1 minute.

Slowly add next 3 ingredients, stirring constantly until boiling and thickened. Reduce heat to medium-low. Simmer, uncovered, for 5 minutes to blend flavours.

Add remaining 3 ingredients. Stir-fry for 2 to 3 minutes until shrimp turn pink. Makes about 7 cups (1.75 L).

1 cup (250 mL): 310 Calories; 14.4 g Total Fat (2.3 g Mono, 1.3 g Poly, 9.5 g Sat); 148 mg Cholesterol; 24 g Carbohydrate; 2 g Fibre; 23 g Protein; 504 mg Sodium

seafood and shell stew

Pasta shells underline the seafood theme of this soup. Saffron, though a little pricey, packs lots of flavour and colour in one pinch. Garnish with Aioli (page 14) and serve with plenty of crusty bread to soak up the broth.

Water	4 cups	1 L
Salt	1/2 tsp.	2.5 mL
Medium shell pasta	1 cup	250 mL
Olive (or cooking) oil	1 tbsp.	15 mL
Medium leeks (white part only), thinly sliced	2	2
Small red pepper, diced	1	1
Garlic cloves, minced (or 1/2 tsp., 2 mL, powder)	2	2
Fennel seed, crushed	1/4 tsp.	1 mL
Can of stewed tomatoes (with juice), chopped	14 oz.	398 mL
Clam tomato beverage	1 cup	250 mL
Water	1 cup	250 mL
Dry (or alcohol-free) white wine	1/2 cup	125 mL
Grated lemon zest	1/2 tsp.	2 mL
Dried thyme, crushed	1/8 tsp.	0.5 mL
Saffron threads (or turmeric), just a pinch		
Uncooked medium shrimp (peeled and deveined), (about 30)	1 lb.	454 g
Cod fillets, bones removed, cut into 1 inch (2.5 cm) cubes	8 oz.	225 g
Halibut fillets, bones removed, cut into 1 inch (2.5 cm) cubes	8 oz.	225 g
Chopped fresh cilantro (optional)	1 tbsp.	15 mL
Chopped fresh parsley (optional)	1 tbsp.	15 mL
Hot pepper sauce (optional)	1/4 – 1/2 tsp.	1 – 2 mL

Combine first amount of water and salt in medium saucepan. Bring to a boil. Add pasta. Boil, uncovered, for about 6 minutes, stirring occasionally, until partially cooked. Drain. Rinse with cold water. Drain. Set aside.

Heat olive oil in large saucepan or Dutch oven on medium. Add next 4 ingredients. Cook, uncovered, for about 5 minutes, stirring often, until leek is softened.

Add next 7 ingredients. Stir. Bring to a boil. Reduce heat to medium. Simmer, covered, for 15 minutes.

Add pasta and remaining 6 ingredients. Stir. Reduce heat to medium-low. Simmer, covered, for about 10 minutes until fish flakes easily when tested with fork and pasta is tender but firm. Makes about 8 cups (2 L).

1 cup (250 mL): 257 Calories; 3.6 g Total Fat (1.6 g Mono, 0.7 g Poly, 0.6 g Sat); 55 mg Cholesterol; 33 g Carbohydrate; 2 g Fibre; 21 g Protein; 290 mg Sodium

shrimp fried rice

Make extra rice one night so you can get a quick start on this fabulous,
Asian-inspired dish. The beaten eggs add a moist, sticky consistency to the rice.
If you'd like cooked egg pieces, add the beaten eggs earlier in the cooking process.

Cooking oil	1 tbsp.	15 mL
Thinly sliced onion	1/2 cup	125 mL
Chopped fresh white mushrooms	1 cup	250 mL
Sliced green onion	1/3 cup	75 mL
Soy sauce	2 tbsp.	30 mL
Ground ginger	1/4 tsp.	1 mL
Salt	1/2 tsp.	2 mL
Pepper, just a pinch		
Cold cooked long grain white rice (about 1 2/3 cups, 400 mL, uncooked)	5 cups	1.25 L
Cooked baby shrimp	1/2 lb.	225 g
Large eggs	2	2
Water	1 1/2 tbsp.	25 mL

Heat large frying pan or wok on medium-high until very hot. Add cooking oil.
Add onion. Sir-fry for about 2 minutes until onion is softened.

Add mushrooms and green onion. Stir-fry for about 2 minutes until mushrooms
are softened and liquid is evaporated.

Add next 4 ingredients. Stir. Add rice. Stir-fry until heated through.

Add shrimp. Stir-fry until heated through.

Beat eggs and water in small bowl. Pour over rice. Stir-fry until eggs begin to set.
Serves 6.

1 serving: 269 Calories; 5.5 g Total Fat (2.3 g Mono,1.3 g Poly, 0.9 g Sat); 119 mg Cholesterol;
40 g Carbohydrate; 1 g Fibre; 14 g Protein; 714 mg Sodium

shrimp casserole

You can assemble this in the morning and refrigerate. Before you leave work that afternoon, call the kids and tell them to pop it into the oven for you.

Fresh asparagus, trimmed of tough ends cut into 1 inch (2.5 cm) pieces (about 4 1/2 cups, 1.1 L)	1 1/2 lbs.	680 g
Large eggs	6	6
Cooked salad shrimp	8 oz.	225 g
Finely chopped green pepper	1/2 cup	125 mL
Finely chopped onion	1/3 cup	75 mL
Garlic powder	1/4 tsp.	1 mL
Salt	1/2 tsp.	2 mL
Pepper	1/4 tsp.	1 mL
Ground thyme, just a pinch		
Grated sharp Cheddar cheese	1 cup	250 mL

Pour water into large frying pan until about 1 inch (2.5 cm) deep. Bring to a boil. Add asparagus. Reduce heat to medium. Cook, covered, for about 4 minutes until tender-crisp. Drain.

Beat eggs in large bowl until frothy. Add next 7 ingredients. Stir. Add asparagus. Stir. Spread in greased 2 quart (2 L) baking dish. Bake in 350°F (175°C) oven for about 40 minutes until set.

Sprinkle with cheese. Bake for another 4 to 6 minutes until cheese is melted. Serves 6.

1 serving: 222 Calories; 12.3 g Total Fat (3.9 g Mono, 1.1 g Poly, 5.9 g Sat); 310 mg Cholesterol; 7 g Carbohydrate; 2 g Fibre; 22 g Protein; 471 mg Sodium

shrimp creole

The bayous of Louisiana have long provided the main ingredient for this Cajun dish. Add more hot sauce if you can stand the heat. Serve this over rice.

Cooking oil	1 tbsp.	15 mL
Chopped celery	1 cup	250 mL
Chopped onion	1 cup	250 mL
Diced green pepper	1 cup	250 mL
Garlic clove, minced (or 1/4 tsp., 1 mL, powder)	1	1
Can of diced tomatoes (with juice)	14 oz.	398 mL
Tomato paste (see Tip, page 64)	2 tbsp.	30 mL
Lemon juice	1 tbsp.	15 mL
Granulated sugar	2 tsp.	10 mL
Bay leaf	1	1
Dried thyme	1/2 tsp.	2 mL
Salt	1/2 tsp.	2 mL
Pepper	1/4 tsp.	1 mL
Louisiana hot sauce (optional)	1 tsp.	5 mL
Uncooked medium shrimp (peeled and deveined), about 60	2 lbs.	900 g

Heat cooking oil in large frying pan on medium. Add next 4 ingredients. Cook for 5 to 10 minutes, stirring often, until onion is softened.

Add next 9 ingredients. Stir. Bring to a boil. Reduce heat to medium-low. Simmer, uncovered, for 10 minutes to blend flavours.

Add shrimp. Bring to a boil. Reduce heat to medium-low. Simmer, uncovered, for about 10 minutes, stirring occasionally, until shrimp turn pink. Makes about 6 3/4 cups (1.7 L). Serves 6.

1 serving: 226 Calories; 5.3 g Total Fat (1.8 g Mono, 1.8 g Poly, 0.7 g Sat); 228 mg Cholesterol; 12 g Carbohydrate; 2 g Fibre; 32 g Protein; 553 mg Sodium

seafood enchiladas

Soft tortillas stuffed with delectably seasoned seafood are topped with salsa and melted cheese. Finish this dish with a tasty Mexican garnish of chopped tomato and avocado.

Uncooked small bay scallops	1 lb.	454 g		Grated medium Cheddar cheese	1 cup	250 mL
Uncooked medium shrimp (peeled and deveined)	3/4 lb.	340 g		Grated Monterey Jack cheese	1 cup	250 mL
Water	1 cup	250 mL				
Block of cream cheese, softened	8 oz.	250 g				
Sour cream	1/2 cup	125 mL				
Chopped yellow pepper	2/3 cup	150 mL				
Sliced green onion	2/3 cup	150 mL				
Can of crabmeat, drained, cartilage removed, flaked	4 1/4 oz.	120 g				
Garlic clove, minced (or 1/4 tsp., 1 mL, powder)	1	1				
Ground cumin	1/2 tsp.	2 mL				
Salt	1/4 tsp.	1 mL				
Pepper	1/4 tsp.	1 mL				
Chopped fresh cilantro or parsley (optional)	2 tbsp.	30 mL				
Flour tortillas (9 inch, 22 cm, diameter)	6	6				
Mild salsa	2 cups	500 mL				

Combine first 3 ingredients in medium saucepan. Bring to a boil. Reduce heat to medium-low. Simmer, covered, for about 2 minutes until scallops are opaque and shrimp turn pink. Drain. Chop. Set aside.

Beat cream cheese and sour cream in large bowl until smooth. Add next 8 ingredients and reserved seafood mixture. Stir.

Spoon seafood mixture across centre of tortillas. Fold sides over filling. Roll up from bottom to enclose. Arrange, seam-side down, in greased 9 x 13 inch (22 x 33 cm) baking dish.

Pour salsa over top. Bake, uncovered, in 375°F (190°C) oven for about 20 minutes until heated through.

Sprinkle with both cheeses. Bake, uncovered, for another 3 to 5 minutes until cheese is melted. Serves 6.

1 serving: 696 Calories; 36.3 g Total Fat (10.5 g Mono, 3.4 g Poly, 19.9 g Sat); 203 mg Cholesterol; 45 g Carbohydrate; 4 g Fibre; 47 g Protein; 1322 mg Sodium

seafood lasagna

Assemble the day before, cover and refrigerate.

Water	12 cups	3 L
Salt	1 1/2 tsp.	7 mL
Lasagna noodles	8	8
Butter (or hard margarine)	2 tbsp.	30 mL
Chopped onion	1 cup	250 mL
Chopped celery	1/4 cup	60 mL
Block of cream cheese, softened, cut up	8 oz.	250 g
Large egg	1	1
2% cottage cheese	1 1/2 cups	375 mL
Grated Parmesan cheese	2 tbsp.	30 mL
Dried basil	2 tsp.	10 mL
Salt	1/2 tsp.	2 mL
Pepper	1/8 tsp.	0.5 mL
Butter (or hard margarine)	1/4 cup	60 mL
All-purpose flour	1/4 cup	60 mL
Salt	1/2 tsp.	2 mL
Pepper	1/8 tsp.	0.5 mL
Milk	2 cups	500 mL
Cans of crabmeat, drained, cartilage removed, flaked (4 1/2 oz., 120 g, each)	2	2
Cooked small shrimp, tails removed	1 cup	250 mL
Dry (or alcohol-free) white wine	1/3 cup	75 mL
Grated Parmesan cheese	1/4 cup	60 mL
Grated Cheddar cheese	1 cup	250 mL

Combine water and salt in Dutch oven. Bring to a boil. Add lasagna noodles. Boil, uncovered, for 12 to 14 minutes, stirring occasionally, until tender but firm. Drain. Rinse with cold water. Drain. Set aside.

Melt first amount of butter in large frying pan on medium. Add onion and celery. Cook for 5 to 10 minutes, stirring often, until onion is softened.

Stir in cream cheese until melted. Remove from heat. Add next 6 ingredients. Stir.

Melt second amount of butter in medium saucepan on medium. Add next 3 ingredients. Heat and stir for 1 minute. Slowly add milk, stirring constantly. Heat and stir until boiling and thickened.

Add next 3 ingredients to milk mixture. Stir.

Layer ingredients in greased 9 x 13 inch (22 x 33 cm) pan as follows:

1. 4 lasagna noodles
2. Cottage cheese mixture
3. 4 lasagna noodles
4. Seafood mixture
5. Parmesan cheese

Bake, uncovered, in 375°F (190°C) oven for 45 to 55 minutes until heated through. Sprinkle with Cheddar cheese. Bake for another 3 to 4 minutes until Cheddar cheese is melted. Let stand for 10 minutes before serving. Serves 8.

1 serving: 472 Calories; 27.3 g Total Fat (7.2 g Mono, 1.1 g Poly, 16.6 g Sat); 189 mg Cholesterol; 23 g Carbohydrate; 1 g Fibre; 31 g Protein; 1266 mg Sodium

creamy seafood sauce

Calorie-counting girlfriends will love you for this extravagant, low-fat sauce, delicious over pasta.

Uncooked medium shrimp (peeled and deveined)	1/2 lb.	225 g
Uncooked small bay scallops	1/2 lb.	225 g
Water	1/2 cup	125 mL
Dry (or alcohol-free) white wine	1/4 cup	60 mL
Seafood (or chicken) bouillon powder	1 tsp.	5 mL
Small broccoli florets	2 cups	500 mL
Sliced fresh white mushrooms	1 cup	250 mL
Small zucchini (with peel), diced	1	1
Garlic clove, minced (or 1/4 tsp., 1 mL, powder)	1	1
Finely chopped red pepper	1/2 cup	125 mL
Medium Roma (plum) tomato, diced	1	1
Green onions, sliced	2	2
Basil pesto	2 tbsp.	30 mL
Can of skim evaporated milk	13 1/2 oz.	385 mL
All-purpose flour	3 tbsp.	50 mL

Combine first 5 ingredients in medium saucepan. Bring to a boil. Reduce heat to medium. Boil gently, uncovered, for about 3 minutes until shrimp turn pink. Do not drain. Transfer scallops and shrimp to small bowl using slotted spoon. Cover to keep warm.

Add next 4 ingredients to liquid in saucepan. Bring to a boil. Reduce heat to medium. Boil gently, covered, for 3 minutes.

Add next 4 ingredients. Stir. Bring to a boil. Reduce heat to medium. Simmer, covered, for 3 minutes.

Stir evaporated milk into flour in small bowl until smooth. Slowly add to vegetable mixture, stirring constantly. Heat and stir until boiling and thickened. Add scallops and shrimp. Stir gently until heated through. Makes about 7 cups (1.75 L).

3/4 cup (175 mL): 125 Calories; 2.4 g Total Fat (1.2 g Mono, trace Poly, trace Sat); 46 mg Cholesterol; 11 g Carbohydrate; 1 g Fibre; 14 g Protein; 204 mg Sodium

recipe index

topical tips

Bacterial prevention: It is important to clean the cutting board and any utensils used to cut raw chicken, fish or meat in hot, soapy water immediately after use. This will prevent bacteria from spreading to other food.

Buying and storing shrimp: Reputable fish stores keep fresh shrimp on, or in, ice. Shrimp should have a clean aroma and should never smell of ammonia. To store, wrap loosely to allow for air circulation and keep in the coldest part of the fridge, preferably on ice. Well wrapped, frosen shrimp will keep for three months.

Tomato paste leftovers: If a recipe calls for less than an entire can of tomato paste, freeze the unopened can for 30 minutes. Open both ends and push the contents through one end. Slice off only what you need. Freeze the remaining paste in a resealable freezer bag or plastic wrap for future use.

Toasting nuts, seeds or coconut: Cooking times will vary for each type of nut, so never toast them together. For small amounts, place ingredient in an ungreased shallow frying pan. Heat on medium for three to five minutes, stirring often, until golden. For larger amounts, spread ingredient evenly in an ungreased shallow pan. Bake in a 350°F (175°C) oven for five to 10 minutes, stirring or shaking often, until golden.

Nutrition Information Guidelines

Each recipe is analyzed using the Canadian Nutrient File from Health Canada, which is based on the United States Department of Agriculture (USDA) Nutrient Database.

- If more than one ingredient is listed (such as "butter or hard margarine"), or if a range is given (1 – 2 tsp., 5 – 10 mL), only the first ingredient or first amount is analyzed.

- For meat, poultry and fish, the serving size per person is based on the recommended 4 oz. (113 g) uncooked weight (without bone), which is 2 – 3 oz. (57 – 85 g) cooked weight (without bone) — approximately the size of a deck of playing cards.

- Milk used is 1% M.F. (milk fat), unless otherwise stated.

- Cooking oil used is canola oil, unless otherwise stated.

- Ingredients indicating "sprinkle," "optional," or "for garnish" are not included in the nutrition information.

- The fat in recipes and combination foods can vary greatly depending on the sources and types of fats used in each specific ingredient. For these reasons, the count of saturated, monounsaturated and polyunsaturated fats may not add up to the total fat content.